EXPL

MYSTERIES OF SPACE

by Gini Douglass

PEARSON

Scott
Foresman

Editorial Offices: Glenview, Illinois • Parsippany, New Jersey • New York, New York
Sales Offices: Needham, Massachusetts • Duluth, Georgia • Glenview, Illinois
Coppell, Texas • Ontario, California • Mesa, Arizona

Photo locators denoted as follows: Top (T), Center (C), Bottom (B), Left (L), Right (R), Background (Bkgd)

Opener: Photo Researchers, Inc.; 1 Photo Researchers, Inc.; 3 ©Stone/Getty Images; 5 Corbis; 7 (T) Color-Pic, Inc., (B) Corbis; 9 (T) Library of Congress, (B) Photo Researchers, Inc.; 10 Roger Ressmeyer/Corbis; 13 (T) NASA, (B) DK Images; 15 (B) Photo Researchers, Inc., (T) NASA; 16 Photo Researchers, Inc.; 19 (T) NASA, (B) Photo Researchers, Inc.; 20 (T) Corbis, (B) NASA; 22 NASA; 23 Corbis

ISBN: 0-328-13501-1

Have you ever gazed up at the night sky and wondered about the mysteries of the universe? For instance, do you ever wonder how big the universe is or what it might be like to travel through space and see far off stars and galaxies up close? Have you ever wanted to know exactly how long it would take to travel to another planet in our solar system? What are you seeing when you spot a shooting star? If you have ever found yourself asking such questions, you will be happy to know that you are not alone. Human beings have been gazing up at the sky and wondering about the mysteries of space since the dawn of time.

Over the past few thousand years, humans have been driven by a need to understand and explain the universe, and this desire to understand the mysteries of the universe is something that comes naturally to us all. You may remember being a small child and asking questions about the way the world works. Perhaps you saw a bird fly by, and you wondered how that was possible. Or, perhaps you wondered why the moon appeared to be round and full on some days, and shaped like a banana on others. We humans are born with a deep sense of curiosity about the world around us, and it is our curiosity that inspires us to learn about the world in which we live.

Just as we are curious about what lies beyond our solar system and our **galaxy,** the Milky Way, early **astronomers** had a strong desire to understand what they were seeing in the sky. Long before technology was available to assist them, early astronomers were able to make accurate guesses about the planets and stars. For example, by observing the positions of the sun and moon in the sky, early astronomers were able to create calendars that were very similar to the calendars we use today, and early astronomers even took the time to map the position of every visible star in the night sky.

Copernicus (top) believed in a heliocentric universe. His diagram shows the Sun as the center of the solar system (bottom).

As early as 280 B.C., a Greek man named Aristarchus suggested that we live in a **heliocentric** universe, with Earth revolving around the sun. Scientists did not accept his views. If Earth was moving, why couldn't they feel it? They believed that the universe was Earth-centered, or **geocentric.**

Over time ideas about space changed. As a result of the work of astronomers such as Nicolaus Copernicus (1473–1543) from Poland, we came back to the sun-centered view of the solar system. When we understood that Earth was not the center of everything, we saw that the universe was much more vast and unknown than we had previously imagined.

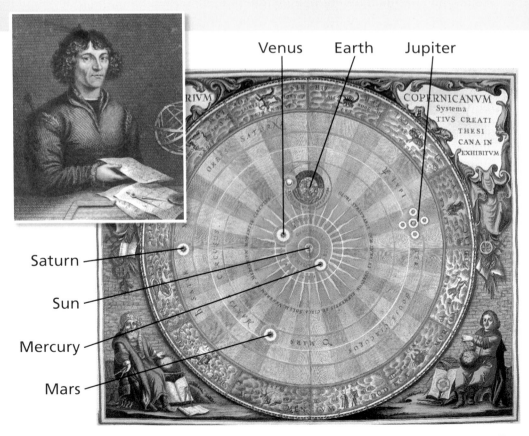

Venus   Earth   Jupiter

Saturn

Sun

Mercury

Mars

As a new view of the universe continued to take shape, another revolutionary event occurred. In 1608 a man from the Netherlands named Hans Lippershey invented the first telescope, called a *kijker,* or "looker." Astronomy would never be the same again, and humanity was on its way to exploring the far distances of space through a telescopic lens. One of the first persons to use a telescope to study space was the Italian astronomer Galileo Galilei. Galileo lived from 1564 to 1642, and he made several important discoveries during his lifetime. Galileo was the first to observe dark spots on the sun called sunspots, and he observed the craters and peaks that exist on the surface of the Moon. By using a telescope, Galileo was also able to prove Copernicus's claim that the planets in our solar system revolved around the sun.

As time went on, astronomers used telescopes to observe space. Astronomers learned more and more about the planets in our solar system, and our idea of space began to take on more and more detail. In 1705 Edmond Halley claimed that comets were in orbit around the sun, and that one in particular would pass by Earth every seventy-six years. It is now called Halley's comet.

Halley's comet (above) and
Edmond Halley (far right)

It turns out that Halley's comet does exist, and its
orbit has been witnessed by many people throughout
history. Today we know that comets are actually made
up of lumps of ice and dust that travel from the outer
areas of the solar system toward its center, the sun.
When comets get closer to the sun, the heat turns the
ice into steam, and the jets of gas they emit form long
tails that can be seen from Earth. Halley's comet made
its most recent appearance in 1986, and a number of
countries sent out spacecraft to snap some photos of
the famous comet. The next chance we will have to see
Halley's comet will be in the year 2062!

When you see a streak of light in the night sky it may appear as if a star is falling toward Earth. What you are actually seeing is a bit of space **debris** called a meteoroid. It is believed that meteoroids are formed when asteroids collide in space. Asteroids are made of rock or metal, and they orbit the sun in a region between Mars and Jupiter called the Asteroid Belt. Italian astronomer Giuseppe Piazzi discovered the first minor planet, or asteroid, called Ceres, in 1801. It was estimated to be 930 km (578 miles) in diameter, which is about the same size as Texas!

The 1800s was an exciting time in the history of astronomy. At this time, astronomers were learning more about the planets and their orbits, or revolutions around the sun, and beginning to understand more about the universe in the process. For example, in 1846, the eighth planet from the sun, Neptune, was discovered.

Scientists figured out that, according to Newton's laws of motion, there was something not quite right about the orbit of Uranus, the seventh planet from the sun. Scientists predicted that another planet, now called Neptune, might exist beyond Uranus, which would explain the disturbance of Uranus's orbit. They were right.

The mathematician and physicist Isaac Newton (top) described how and why objects move in his three rules known as Newton's laws of motion. His work helped scientists discover the planet Neptune (bottom).

Neptune was actually observed in 1612 by Galileo. Galileo observed Neptune, but he concluded that the enormous blue object was a star rather than a planet. During the few days that Galileo had the opportunity to observe Neptune, he noticed that its position seemed to change slightly. Ordinarily, this might have suggested to him that what he observed was something other than a star, but unfortunately, Neptune slipped out of his view before he could determine that it was indeed a planet and not a star. Of course, we now know that there is only one star in our solar system: the sun.

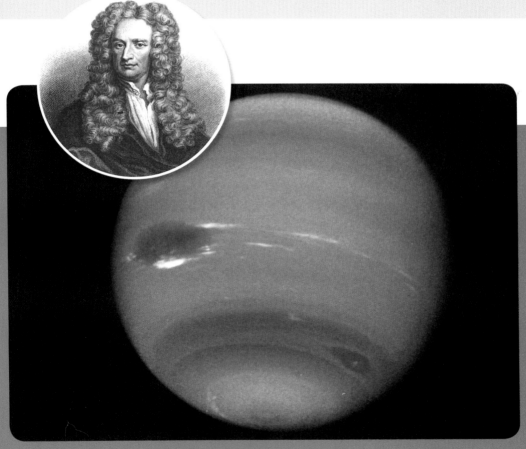

The case of Galileo's near discovery of a new planet shows how much our understanding of the solar system and outer space has changed in only a few centuries. In fact, astronomers at the beginning of the 1900s were not aware that any galaxies beyond our own galaxy, the Milky Way galaxy, existed.

This is the W. M. Keck Observatory in Hawaii (left) and an interior view of its telescope (below).

Astronomers began to notice what looked like cloudy patches of distant stars, and they concluded that these patches were part of the Milky Way galaxy. In the 1920s a man named Edwin Hubble studied these same patches of stars, and he realized that he was, in fact, observing other galaxies!

Astronomers and scientists in the 1900s continued to observe and study the mysteries of space. These scientists used powerful telescopes to search for far-off planets and stars, and they also began to understand that new forms of space exploration were possible. Soon, they began to develop the technology that would make space exploration a reality.

The technological advances of the 1900s brought about a new effort to explore deep into space, and modern space exploration took on a whole new dimension. Up until that time period, our exploration of space was limited to what we could observe from Earth. Though we learned a great deal about space from what we observed through powerful modern telescopes, scientists and astronomers knew that we could learn even more by traveling through space itself. If we could find a way to get beyond Earth's atmosphere, then we could gain a whole new perspective of our solar system and outer space.

It soon became evident that rockets were the secret to making space exploration possible. As early as A.D. 1045, the Chinese had used rockets for military purposes. A Russian scientist named Konstantin Tsiolkovsky, who lived in the mid-1800s to early 1900s, had made important discoveries regarding rocket science and space flight. Tsiolkovsky's discoveries were essential to our understanding of how rockets could be used to launch space ships.

In 1919 an American scientist named Robert Goddard began to experiment with rockets. Goddard was the first to suggest that a rocket could one day reach the moon. Many people made fun of Goddard and his ideas, but history would soon prove that his ideas were not so crazy after all.

Goddard worked with the U.S. government during World War II, using the rocket technology he developed to aid in the war effort. At the same time, scientists in other countries worked to develop their own programs in rocket science. In 1957 the Soviet Union (now called Russia) launched the world's first man-made **satellite,** Sputnik 1, into orbit around Earth. A few months later, the United States launched its own satellite, Explorer 1, into space.

NASA was created partly in response to the successful launch of Sputnik 1 (above) and the Russian space program.

In 1958 a very important, government-sponsored organization called the National Aeronautics and Space Administration (NASA) came into being. NASA became the center of technological and scientific research for the American space program and remains its headquarters today. NASA was established, in part, in response to the successful launch of the satellite Sputnik 1 by the Soviet Union. In the years following World War II, the governments of the United States and the Soviet Union did not have a good relationship, and the two countries each lived in fear that the other would move ahead in the race to explore space.

13

Although relations were not very good, the competition between the Soviet Union and the United States inspired each country to make great progress in space exploration. Achieving human space travel became a priority for both nations, and NASA's goal was to make human space travel a reality. Just twelve years after the launch of Sputnik 1, the United States sent astronauts to the moon.

The United States and Soviet Union continued to launch more satellites and robotic aircraft into space, and the dream of sending a human being into space would soon become a reality. Before this could be accomplished, however, it was important that unmanned missions collect as much information as possible about the conditions humans would face during space travel.

Unmanned missions into space have brought back crucial information that allowed us to prepare for human space flight. Sending an unmanned aircraft or satellite into space has many benefits. Unmanned (or robotic) spacecraft and satellites can go farther into space and can remain in space for longer periods than spacecraft carrying humans. Also, since there is no need to worry about supporting and protecting human life, the level of risk is much lower.

Unmanned aircraft and satellites were very important to both space programs at the time, and they continue to be essential to space programs today. For instance, even though the technology we have created has allowed us to travel to the moon, we are still unable to travel to the surface of the planet Mars. For human beings, the trip still would be too risky. Our technology has not caught up with our dream to visit another planet in person, which is why robotic missions are so important.

A Mars Rover collects information and takes photos of the red planet's surface.

Over the past four decades, other important unmanned space missions have brought back astonishing pictures of the distant places in our solar system and beyond. The Hubble Space Telescope, named after the astronomer Edwin Hubble, was launched into space in 1990. NASA and the European Space Agency (ESA) created and designed the Hubble together. The Hubble Telescope is actually a floating observatory, orbiting Earth at the rate of five miles per second. It takes the Hubble telescope only ninety-six minutes to make one complete orbit of Earth.

These images of nebulae were photographed by the Hubble.

The satellite Galileo, which was launched into space in 1989 by the space shuttle Atlantis, provided us with more evidence that our solar system is a mysterious and enchanting place. Galileo's mission was to travel to the planet Jupiter. Once it arrived, after traveling more than six years, the satellite collected **data** about Jupiter and some of its moons. It was hoped that Galileo's mission would last for about two years, but the hardworking satellite ended up sticking around for eight! As a result of Galileo's mission, we were able to learn more information than ever before about Jupiter's atmosphere and about some of Jupiter's moons.

Unmanned missions into space continue to be an essential aspect of our space program, and scientists are currently hard at work designing new spacecraft and planning new missions that will stretch the boundaries of our imaginations even further. These unmanned missions have taught us that we are but a small piece of the puzzle that is the universe.

Nevertheless, what we lack in size, we make up for in spirit. The information we have learned about our universe at each step of our space program has motivated us to continue our exploration, and human space travel has been, perhaps, the most dramatic and inspiring form of space exploration to date.

Many people have volunteered to take the giant leap into outer space. It all began in 1961, four years after the Soviet launch of Sputnik 1. The first person to travel to outer space was a Russian man named Yuri Gagarin. Gagarin orbited Earth once in a spacecraft called the Vostok 1, and his flight lasted one hour and twenty-nine minutes. Today, astronauts are able to stay in space for much longer, but back in 1961, Gagarin's mission was nothing short of miraculous.

After Yuri Gagarin's trip, an American astronaut named Alan B. Shepard, Jr., became the second human being, and the first American, to orbit Earth. Following these two moments in space history, the race between the Soviet Union and the United States intensified. While the Soviet Union seemed to be more interested in doing scientific research in space, the United States was determined to send the first human being to the moon. This became the main focus of our space program, and a matter of national interest.

In 1961 President John F. Kennedy challenged the American people to put a man on the moon by the end of the decade. Kennedy inspired the nation, especially the many dedicated people at NASA who worked, through trial and error, to make this dream a reality.

The Apollo 11 crew (right) and the first steps on the moon (above)

In 1967 NASA began a series of missions into space called the Apollo missions. In 1969, after learning as much as possible about how to travel safely on the moon, NASA launched the Apollo 11 mission. On July 20, astronauts Neil A. Armstrong and Edwin E. Aldrin, Jr., landed safely on the moon's surface in a lunar module designed to carry them to their destination. Millions of people back on Earth watched the incredible events unfold on TV.

It has been called one of the most important moments in human history. Armstrong, commander of the Apollo 11 mission, became the first man to walk on the moon. His words upon setting foot on the lunar surface were, "That's one small step for man, one giant leap for mankind." Today, Armstrong's words remain as unforgettable as the triumphant success of the Apollo 11 mission.

Armstrong and Aldrin's visit to the moon lasted a little longer than two hours, but the effect of their visit on the imagination of the American people and the world would last much longer. Following the success of the Apollo 11 mission, we continued to strive to reach new heights in space.

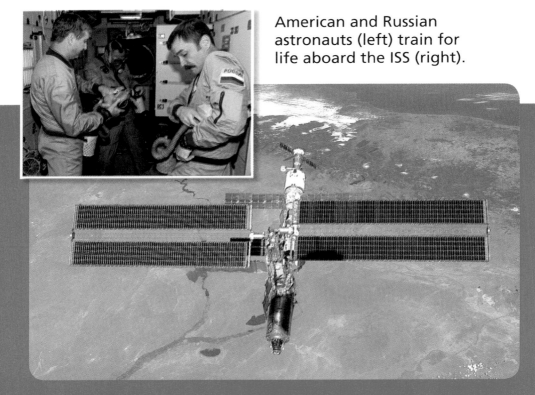

American and Russian astronauts (left) train for life aboard the ISS (right).

Human space exploration is still a relatively new enterprise, but it is amazing to consider the progress we have made. We must pay tribute to the many brave astronauts who have risked their own safety so that humankind could benefit from their brilliant work in space. Today, human space exploration has become a truly international effort, and people from many different countries have contributed their ideas and knowledge to the cause of space exploration.

Russia and the United States, along with fourteen other countries, are working together to complete the International Space Station (ISS). The International Space Station is large enough for astronauts to live and work inside it. The first piece of the station was launched in November of 1998, and since then many sections have been added to it–it is currently the length of three school buses. By the time it is completed, it will be about the length of a football field. Scientists hope that their work at the ISS will bring us closer to our goal of visiting and living on a planet such as Mars.

Human beings have never stopped striving to learn more and more about our place in the universe. The more we learn, the more we realize how much is still unknown to us. People once believed that the planet Earth was the center of the universe, but we now understand that it is a tiny part of a vast universe yet to be explored.

Now Try This

Lead a Mission to the International Space Station

Now it's your turn to go on a mission into space—a mission of the imagination. At this very moment on the International Space Station, a crew of astronauts is hard at work conducting experiments and helping with its construction. By the time construction on the Space Station is completed, it will have taken forty-five missions to get the job done.

Several crews on many different missions have already traveled to the International Space Station to contribute their skills toward its completion. Teamwork has been the key to making these missions possible. If you could be the commander of the next mission to the International Space Station, what would you like to say to your crew? Why not start by writing a letter of welcome!

1. First, before you sit down to write your letter of welcome, you may want to take some time to brainstorm. What are the most important points you want to make?

2. You may want to mention some important moments in the history of space exploration in order to inspire your crew. Think about some of the exciting discoveries and missions that have taken place in the past. What do you think was the most inspiring moment in space exploration history?

3. You may want to thank your crew for joining you on this mission, and congratulate them on their success as astronauts. Be sure to tell them how much you will appreciate their hard work.

4. As you may know, space missions always have powerful and memorable names. Some of the earlier space missions have had names such as Mercury, Apollo, and Endeavor. If you could choose an inspiring name for your mission, what would it be? How will this name reflect the goals of your mission to work at the International Space Station?

Glossary

astronomers *n.* experts in the science that deals with the sun, moon, planets, stars, etc.

data *n.* facts from which conclusions can be drawn; things known or admitted; information.

debris *n.* scattered fragments; ruins; rubbish.

galaxy *n.* a group of billions of stars forming one system.

geocentric *adj.* viewed or measured from Earth's center.

heliocentric *adj.* with the sun at the center.

satellite *n.* an astronomical object that revolves around a planet; a moon.